All rights reserved, no part of this publication may be either reproduced or transmitted by any means whatsoever without the prior permission of the publisher.

Text and Images © Charlotte E Moore

GINGER FYRE PRESS

Gingerfyrepress.com

Typesetting © Ginger Fyre Press

July 2021

Ginger Fyre Press is an imprint of Veneficia Publications

The Life of a Large Blue Butterfly

Written and Illustrated

by

Charlotte E Moore

This book belongs to

_____

Hello, my name is Barnaby. Come and join me on a journey through my life . . .

One warm sunny morning in a meadow full of life and colour, a butterfly called a Large Blue laid her eggs. The eggs were laid underneath the small purple flowers of a plant called wild thyme.

LARGE BLUE BUTTERFLY FACTS

Butterflies lay around a thousand eggs, where they feel it is safe for the unhatched caterpillars. But not all of the eggs hatch and of those that do, only a few survive. This is one of the reasons why butterflies lay so many eggs.

Butterflies often lay their eggs on leaves or foods that are suitable for the caterpillars to eat as their first food once they have hatched.

Large Blue Butterflies are one of the rarest butterflies and during the summer months, they lay their eggs on wild thyme which grows on dry, dusty soil.

A few days later, the mother butterfly's eggs began to hatch. One by one, small caterpillars began to come out of their hard shells. They were curious at all the sights around them, and the meadow looked so big. But they were also very hungry.

LARGE BLUE BUTTERFLY FACTS

Like many caterpillars, when Large Blue Butterfly caterpillars hatch, they will eat their eggshell.

They will also feed from the seeds of the wild thyme flowers before moving onto vegetation around them, such as the leaves of the wild thyme.

As the days and weeks passed, the small caterpillars hatched and lived on the wild thyme. Then as one caterpillar continued to eat the seeds and the surrounding leaves, he fell to the meadow floor.

All around the little caterpillar, was a meadow full of wonder and beauty, but it was also a very big world for the little caterpillar too. However, the caterpillar wasn't alone for long and was soon spotted by some nearby ants.

LARGE BLUE BUTTERFLY FACTS

Large Blue Butterflies often lay their eggs in a meadow which has dry soil. These meadows are also home to hundreds of red ants.

Large Blue Butterfly caterpillars are a reddish brown colour and smell just like red ant larva. This makes the ants believe that the caterpillar has accidently come out of the ants nest, so it will be taken back to the nest by the forager ants.

Before the little caterpillar knew it, he was being carried by a group of red ants away from where he had just fallen to the ground.

"W - w - what's going on? Where are you taking me?" The little caterpillar nervously asked.

"It's ok, little one. You have come out of our nest, so we are taking you back to where you belong," a forager ant explained.

LARGE BLUE BUTTERFLY FACTS

In an ants' nest there are worker ants that have the job of looking after the new ant babies called larvae in the nursery chamber.

The Large Blue Butterflies are bigger than the ants' larvae and are also a completely different colour. But the caterpillars produce a smell called pheromone which is exactly like the smell of the ant larvae.

This makes the ants treat the caterpillars as if they were young ant larvae too.

As soon as they arrived, the curious little caterpillar was handed over to the worker ants that were looking after the new ant larvae.

For the next few weeks, the little caterpillar continued to live amongst the other ants. He was fed and cleaned just like the others and was given his own name - Barnaby.

Barnaby was very happy, and unaware that he was not an ant, and the ants continued to believe that he was one of them.

LARGE BLUE BUTTERFLY FACTS

The caterpillars found by the ants even make the same sounds as the ant larvae, when they are demanding to be fed by the worker ants.

During the next few weeks, more and more Large Blue Butterfly caterpillars are found and brought back to the nest.

One day there was an invader – a wasp. The wasp was not welcome in the nest and the worker ants guarding the ants nest tried everything to stop the wasp from getting in any further.

Suddenly, the wasp released a smell which made the ants begin to fight one another as if they were the enemy. In all the confusion the wasp was able to go further into the nursery!

LARGE BLUE BUTTERFLY FACTS

An insect called an Ichneumon wasp can protect itself against the ants, and trick them into fighting each other. It does this for a special reason; it wants the ants to look after its young, just like they do with the caterpillars.

The wasp knows which ants' nests have Large Blue Butterfly caterpillars inside.

When the wasp attacks the nest, the ants will try to fight it off. This can change in seconds though, as the wasp releases its own pheromone. This smell confuses the ants and makes them fight each other instead of the invader!

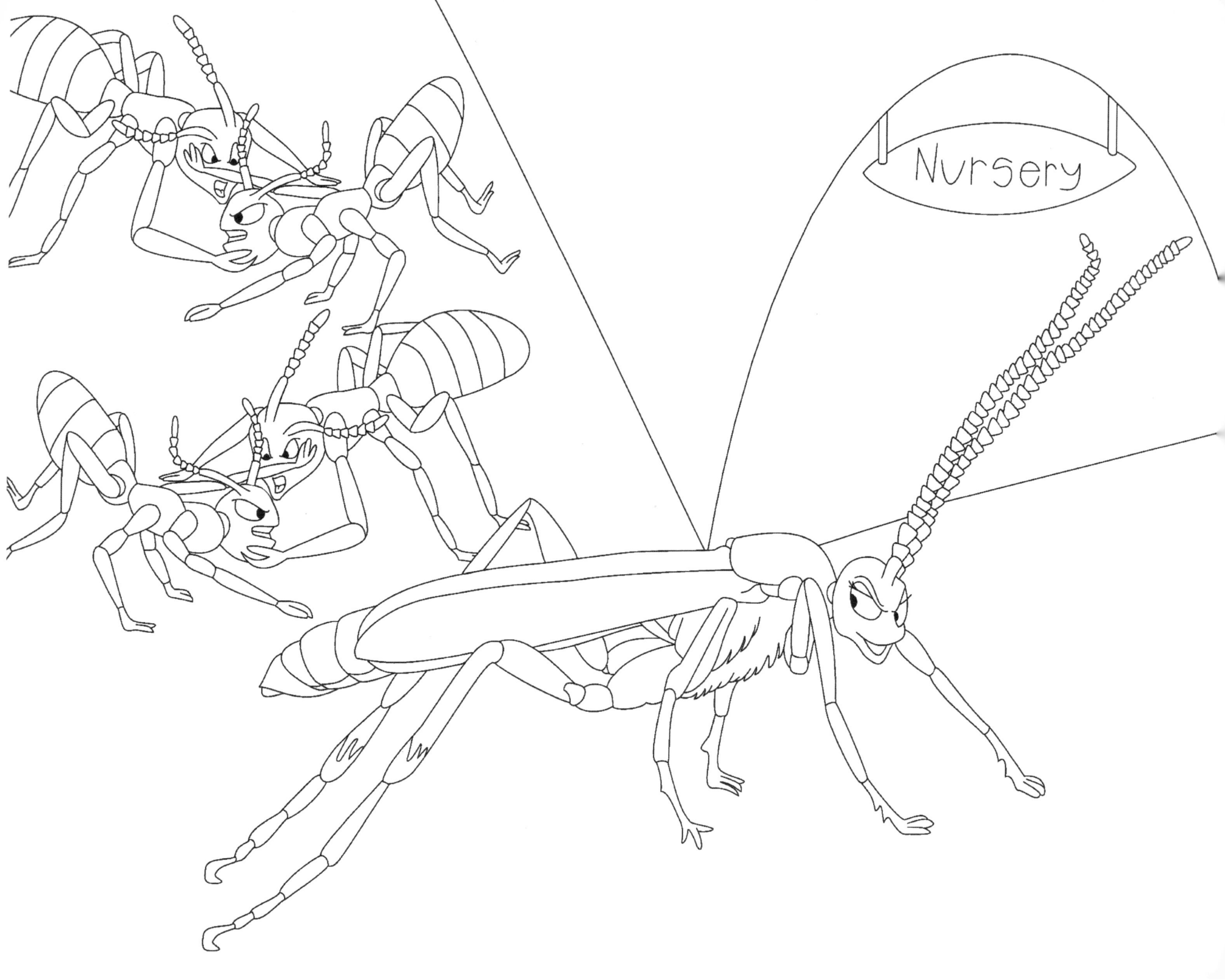

When the wasp entered the nursery, it could easily spot all the Large Blue Butterfly caterpillars because they were reddish brown in colour and stood out from the rest of the ant babies.

But Barnaby, who was nearby saw that there was something wrong; the unusual creature, which didn't seem to look anything like any of the ants, wasn't being very friendly.

"Hey, you're not an ant, leave them alone," Barnaby bravely said to the wasp, who stopped what she was doing and turned to face Barnaby.

"Neither are you, little one," the wasp sneered. This confused Barnaby, but he didn't think much of it and decided to ignore the bully.

LARGE BLUE BUTTERFLY FACTS

With the caterpillars defenceless, the wasp is able to inject each of them with an egg.

Whilst most of the ants continue to fight one another, the wasp will continue to lay eggs in the caterpillars. However, the wasp will only have a certain amount of eggs to lay, so not all of the caterpillars will be affected.

Those caterpillars that aren't affected can continue to grow just like any other caterpillar, shedding their skin as they get bigger.

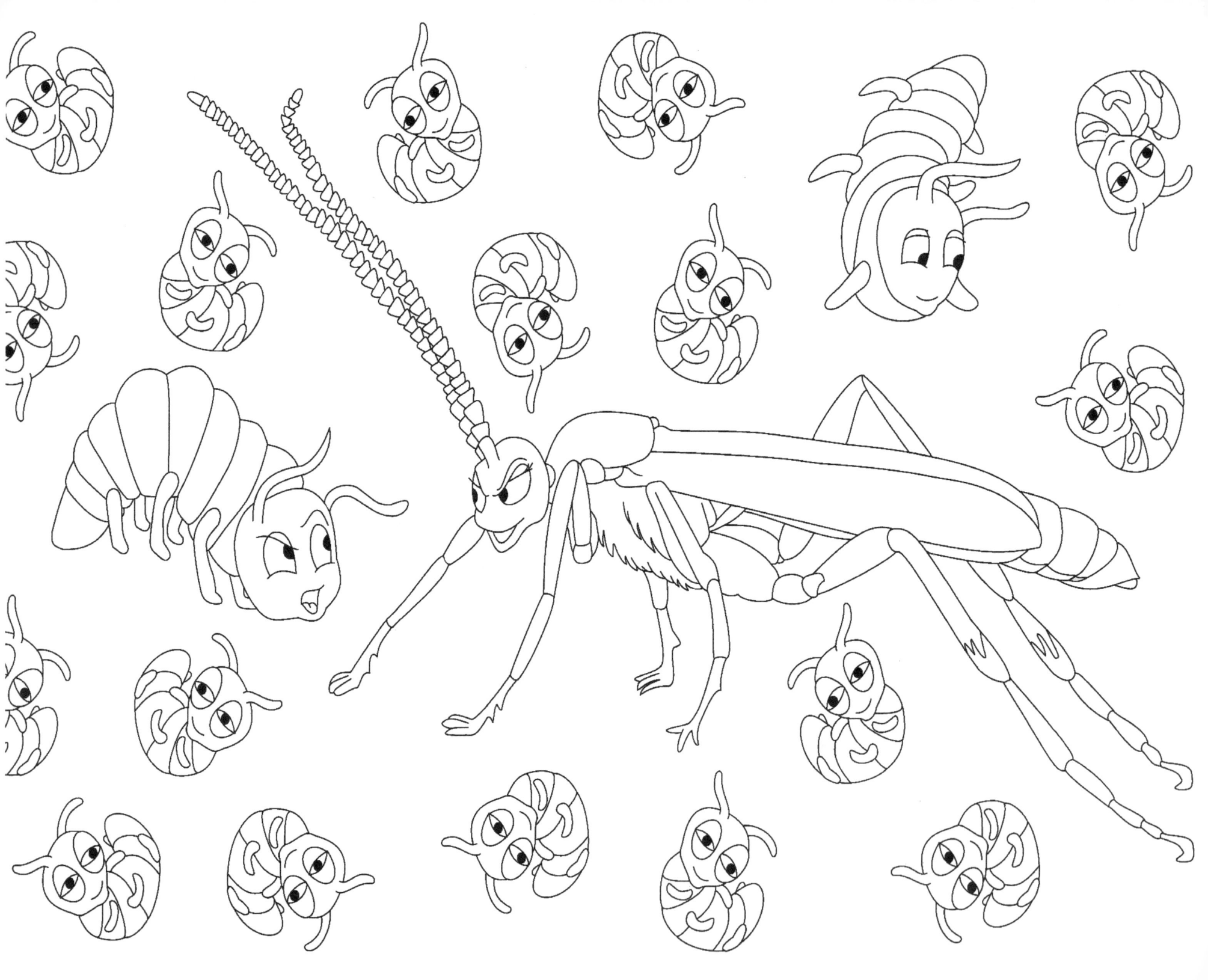

The wasp began to show Barnaby that she was much bigger than Barnaby and tried to scare him.

"I'm not scared of you," Barnaby said to the mean wasp who was trying to bully him.

Then, as the rest of the ants slowly returned back to normal and stopped fighting one another, they were able to force the wasp away from the nursery and back out of the nest.

The caterpillars were saved, thanks to the ants, and to brave Barnaby.

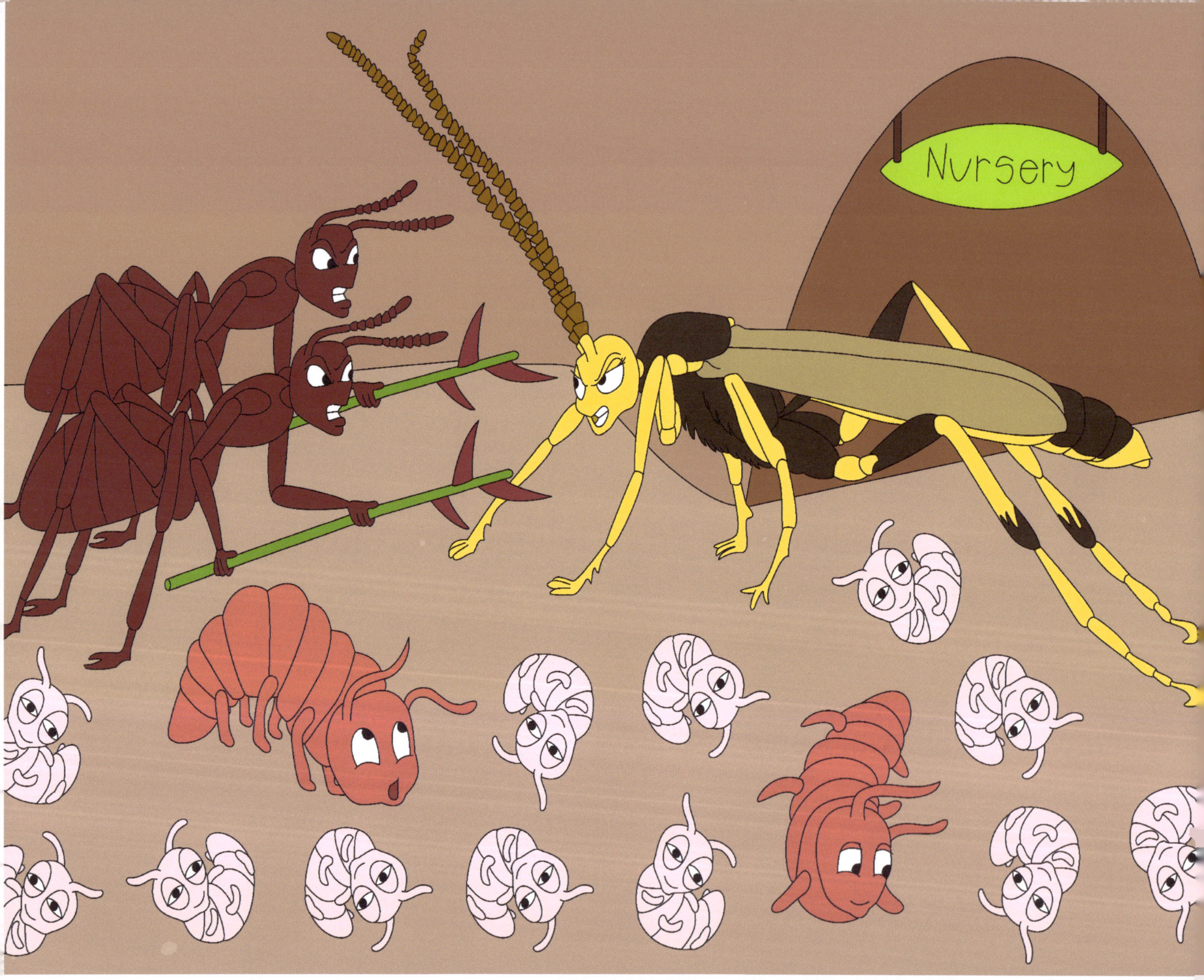

LARGE BLUE BUTTERFLY FACTS

As soon as the wasp has finished injecting her eggs into the caterpillars, the wasp will then leave the ant nest. Unfortunately for these caterpillars there is now a growing wasp larvae inside them which begins to grow and feed on the caterpillar.

When the wasp leaves, so does the pheromone smell. With this gone, the ant colony will slowly return back to normal, allowing the worker ants to continue to care for the caterpillars and the ant larvae.

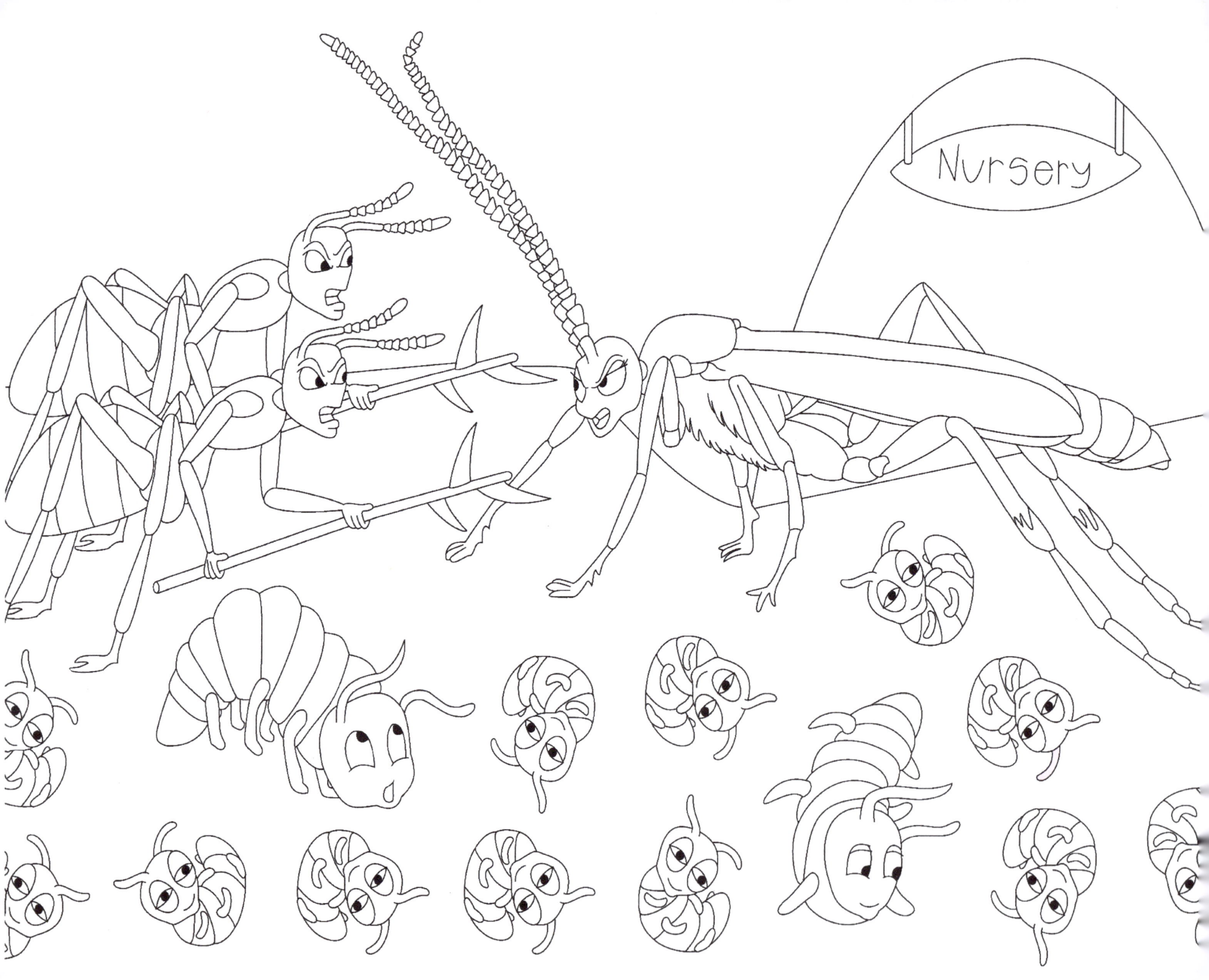

Before Barnaby knew it, many days had passed since the evil wasp tried to attack him and the other caterpillars.

Barnaby wasn't very little anymore. He had become fully grown and was now strong enough to start working for the colony, just like the other ants.

However, Barnaby wasn't an ant, so instead of starting to work, he began to build a hard shell called a chrysalis around himself.

LARGE BLUE BUTTERFLY FACTS

Once the caterpillars are fully grown, they will begin to construct a chrysalis, something that all butterfly caterpillars need to protect themselves, while they turn into an adult.

The chrysalis is made up of the caterpillar's skin, which it sheds for the last time.

This final skin is harder than the previous skins it has shed and forms a tough shell around the caterpillar.

Because Barnaby was now inside his chrysalis, the ants once again thought he was one of their babies that had not yet hatched. So, they cleaned and protected his chrysalis.

Many months later, Barnaby's chrysalis began to hatch, just as many other chrysalises were hatching too. When he had completely hatched, he could see that he wasn't a caterpillar anymore, but a greyish brown creature with beautiful blue wings.

LARGE BLUE BUTTERFLY FACTS

Each chrysalis is cleaned and protected by the ants as if it were one of their own growing adults, until finally they begin to hatch.

"What am I? I don't look like an ant anymore," Barnaby asked a nearby forager ant.

"Yes, you're right. I don't know what you are, but I'm sure you'll soon find out, when you follow them," said the forager ant who pointed to some blue insects just like Barnaby, flying out one of the entrances to the ant hill.

LARGE BLUE BUTTERFLY FACTS

The Large Blue Butterflies that successfully hatch, will leave the ants' nest to extend their butterfly wings out in the open. Now each butterfly is ready to fly, mate and lay eggs, just like its parents did.

The ants back in the nursery chamber will continue to crawl over the hatched chrysalis. This is because they can still smell traces of pheromone, on the empty shell left behind by the butterfly.

The ants will be left puzzled as they no longer have a growing larva, but they will continue to look after the butterflies that have not yet come out of their chrysalis.

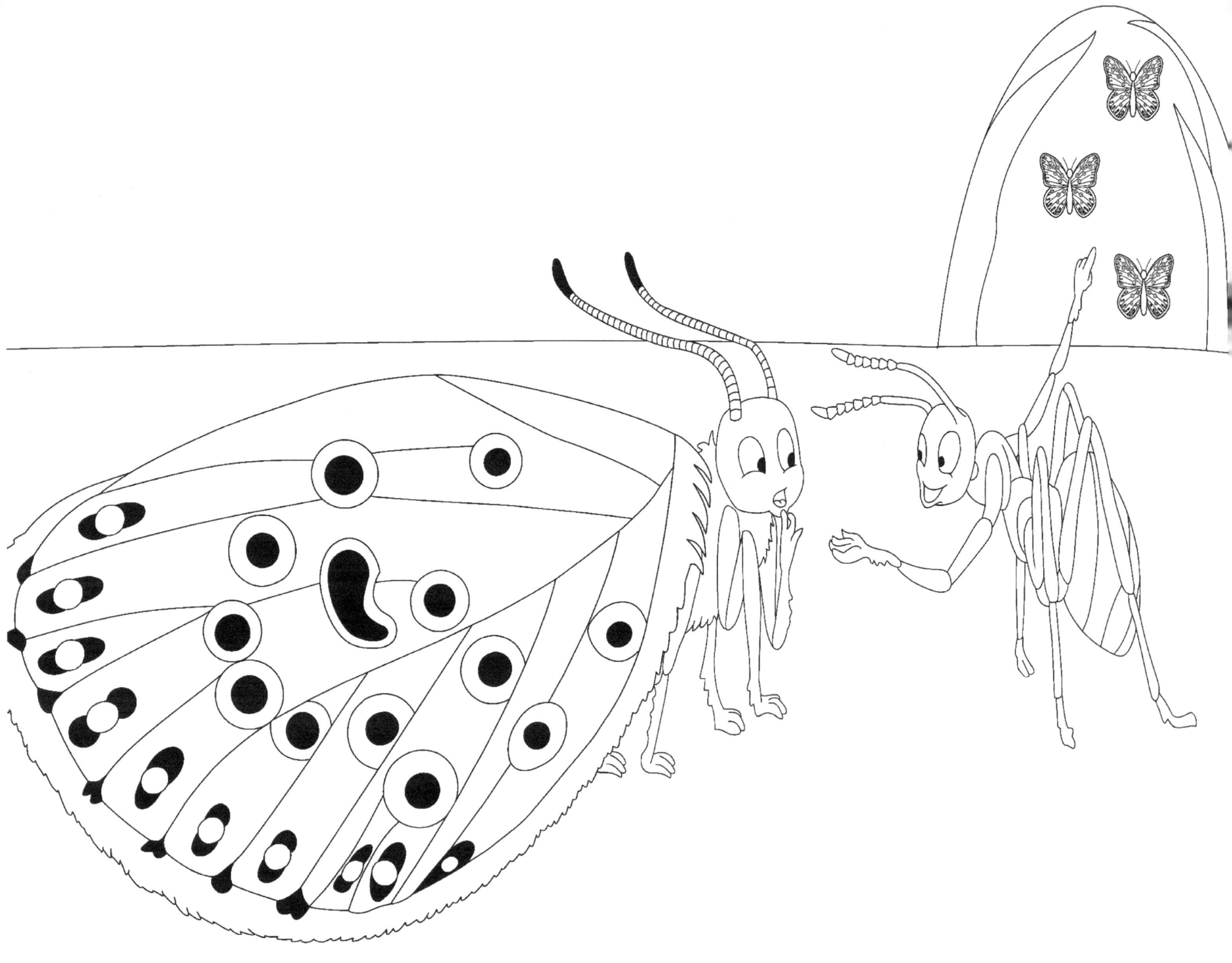

Soon it was Barnaby's time to leave the nest. As he waved goodbye with a smile, Barnaby headed out of the entrance of the nest and went off to discover what type of insect he was.

He was soon flying for the first time. Then, just as he wondered what he was, another young flying blue insect that looked just like him told him that they were Large Blue Butterflies – although, they were still very small compared to the big world.

So, Barnaby followed his new friend and the other Large Blues through the beautiful meadow.

LARGE BLUE BUTTERFLY FACTS

As a new butterfly, a Large Blue will come out of the ant hill, climb up a stem or some grass and then stretch out its new wings.

The new butterfly will search for food, explore, and even fly around. The butterfly may also follow other Large Blue Butterflies.

Barnaby couldn't believe what was above him the whole time. The world was so beautiful. He flew up above the meadow to look down below at his old ant hill home.

"Thank you for looking after me," Barnaby said with a smile.

LARGE BLUE BUTTERFLY FACTS

After a Large Blue Butterfly has flown around the meadow, it will find a mate and the life cycle of the Large Blue Butterfly will start all over again.

Printed in the UK
by
CLOC Book Print
clocbookprint.co.uk

www.ingramcontent.com/pod-product-compliance
Lightning Source LLC
Chambersburg PA
CBHW041819080526

44588CB00004B/64